Body Coverings

# Shells

Cassie Mayer

Heinemann Library
Chicago, Illinois

Photo research by Tracy Cummins and Erica Newbery
Designed by Jo Hinton-Malivoire
Printed and bound in China by South China Printing Company
10 09 08
10 9 8 7 6 5 4 3 2

**Library of Congress Cataloging-in-Publication Data**
Mayer, Cassie.
  Shells / Cassie Mayer.-- 1st ed.
    p. cm. -- (Body coverings)
  Includes bibliographical references and index.
  ISBN 1-4034-8375-2 (hc) -- ISBN 1-4034-8381-7 (pb)
  ISBN 978-1-4034-8375-1 (hc) -- ISBN 978-1-4034-8381-2 (pb)
  1. Shells--Juvenile literature.  I. Title.  II. Series.
  QL405.2.M39 2006
  573.7'7--dc22

                        2005035409

**Acknowledgments**
The author and publisher are grateful to the following for permission to reproduce copyright material:
Corbis pp. **4** (rhino, Royalty Free), **6** (Martin Harvey), **7** and **8** (Jeffrey L. Rotman), **13** and **14** (Sally A. Morgan/Ecoscene), **15** and **16** (Brownie Harris), **20** (Kevin Dodge), **22** (oyster, Louie Psihoyos); Getty Images/Digital Vision p. **4** (kingfisher, leopard); Getty Images/PhotoDisc pp. **4** (lizard), **5**, **23** (snail); Nature Picture Library pp. **11** (Jurgen Freund), **12** (Jurgen Freund), **17** (Pete Oxford), **18** (Pete Oxford), **23** (tortoise, Pete Oxford); Seapics pp. **9**, **10**, **22** (horse shoe crab and hermit crab).

Cover photograph of shells, reproduced with permission of Getty Images/Brand X Pictures. Back cover image of crab reproduced with permission of Seapics.

Special thanks to the Smithsonian Institution and Gary E. Davis for their help with this project.

Every effort has been made to contact copyright holders of any material reproduced in this book. Any omissions will be rectified in subsequent printings if notice is given to the publisher.

# Contents

feathers

fur

scales

skin

Animals have body coverings.
Body coverings protect animals.

shell

Shells are a body covering.

Some animals live inside a shell.

Shells can be smooth.
What animal is this?

shell

snail

This animal is a type of snail.
It is called a cowrie.

Shells can have bumps.
What animal is this?

This animal is a crab.
Its shell covers its whole body.

Shells can be big.
What animal is this?

This animal is a giant clam.
Clams have two shells.

Shells can be small.
What animal is this?

barnacle

This animal is a barnacle.
Barnacles can grow on rocks.

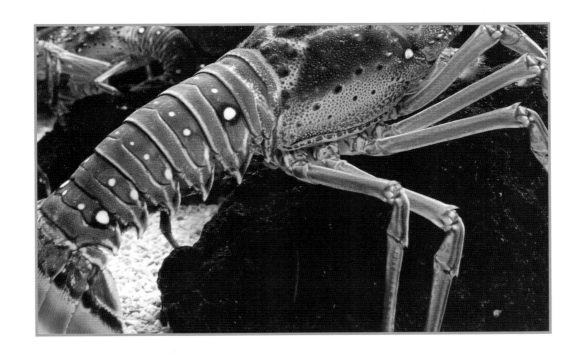

Shells can be bright colors.
What animal is this?

This animal is a lobster.
Its shell can bend.

Shells can have patterns.
What animal is this?

This animal is a tortoise.
Its shell helps it hide.

Do you have a shell?

No, you do not have a shell!
You have skin.

What if you had a shell?
What would your shell be like?

# Fun Shell Facts

Horseshoe crabs have been on the earth for millions of years.

Hermit crabs find their shells.

Oysters create pearls. Pearls are used to make jewelry.

# Picture Glossary

 **pattern** a shape or color that repeats over and over again. Patterns help some animals hide.

 **shell** a type of body covering. Many animals with shells live in the sea.

# Index

**Note to Parents and Teachers**

In this book, children explore characteristics of shells and are introduced to a variety of animals that use this covering for protection. Visual clues and the repetitive question, "What animal is this?" engage children by providing a predictable structure from which to learn new information. The text has been chosen with the advice of a literacy expert to enable beginning readers success while reading independently or with moderate support. Scientists were consulted to provide both interesting and accurate content.

The book ends with an open-ended question that asks children to relate the material to their lives. Use this question as a writing or discussion prompt to encourage creative thinking and assess comprehension. You can also support children's nonfiction literacy skills by helping them to use the table of contents, picture glossary, and index.